Burgers and Bugs

THE SCIENCE BEHIND FOOD

Illustrated by Christopher Masters

PICCOLO
PAN MACMILLAN
CHILDREN'S BOOKS

Also by Lesley Newson in Piccolo

FEELING AWFUL
THE INSIDE STORY

First published 1984 by A. & C. Black Ltd
This Piccolo edition published 1991 by Pan Books Ltd,
Cavaye Place, London SW10 9PG
1 3 5 7 9 8 6 4 2
Text © Lesley Newson 1984
Illustrations © Christopher Masters 1984
ISBN 0 330 31990 6
Printed in England by Clays Ltd, St Ives plc

This book is sold subject to the condition that it shall not,
by way of trade or otherwise, be lent, re-sold, hired out,
or otherwise circulated without the publisher's prior consent
in any form of binding or cover other than that in which
it is published and without a similar condition including this
condition being imposed on the subsequent purchaser

Contents

Food	4
What should we eat?	7
What food is made of	8
Molecules	10
Digestion	11
Getting energy from food	14
Counting Calories	17
The molecules building the body	20
What makes food nutritious?	22
Protein	23
What makes protein?	26
Take the white of an egg	28
Carbohydrates	31
The carbohydrate manufacturing plant	32
Carbohydrate that isn't food	33
Carbohydrate that is food	35
How to find starch	36
Cooking carbohydrates	38
Eating carbohydrates	43
Fat	44
Minerals	47
Vitamins	50
Water	54
Why does food go bad?	56
How to stop food going bad	58
How to eat well	63
Index	64

Food

If you went on a big shopping spree and bought all the food you'd be eating in the next year, you'd need a small fleet of cars to carry it home. The food would probably weigh nearly as much as a car.

You'd have meat, fruit, vegetables and many other kinds of food. Some of the food would be fresh, some frozen, some tinned and some wrapped in cellophane.

You will be eating some of this food because you like it. Some you won't be so keen on, but you'll have to eat it because someone says it's good for you. If you bought a whole year's supply of food in one go, a lot of it would go bad before you had a chance to eat it. If you did try to eat it, it would make you sick.

If you're like most people, you spend a lot of time thinking about food. This isn't surprising because food is one of the most important things in life. Without food we would die.

Some people have to worry about whether they'll be able to get enough food to live on. Other people have far more food than they need; they worry about whether the food tastes good, if it's good for them, or if it's cooked properly.

For thousands of years, people have wondered what food is made of and what happens to food once it is inside us. They've tried to find out if illnesses are caused by the lack of some kinds of food or too much of other kinds.

Scientists now think they can answer many of these questions. They've found out what food is made of and what happens to it in the body. And they also have a fair idea of the sorts of food we need to keep us healthy.

What should we eat?

Many people think that, after all this careful study, scientists should be able to tell us *exactly* what to eat. They would like a sort of recipe for perfect health: two different vegetables a day, one piece of fruit, no more than one and a half chocolate biscuits, three pieces of brown bread . . .

But it isn't that simple.

Think about the kinds of food people eat in different parts of the world. Many people eat food that is quite different from the food we eat, but they are still healthy. There is no doubt that eating meat is good for you. But millions of people in the world have never eaten meat because they believe killing animals is wrong; yet they remain perfectly healthy.

There were also some people who had very little to eat except meat and fish. In regions near the North Pole, very few plants can grow and, until about 100 years ago, many of the people living there had to survive only on the animals they could hunt or catch. They usually ate this meat uncooked.

In some countries, people live mostly on vegetables like manioc or cassava, which you may never have tasted. They may also eat insects which you probably wouldn't even consider tasting. These people may not be as healthy as you, but they can survive on this diet.

How is it possible for people to live on such different kinds of food? Scientists now know it's because the exact sort of food we eat isn't important. All that matters is that the food is made of the right sort of materials.

What food is made of

To get some idea of the sort of things that go into food, you can look at the 'Ingredients' on packages and tins.

A tin of baked beans contains: beans, tomatoes, sugar, salt, food starch, vinegar and spices. These ingredients give the baked beans their special taste. They also contain substances which the body will be able to use once the baked beans have been eaten.

Food scientists have analysed thousands of different sorts of foods – perhaps nearly every kind of food there is. They have found out exactly which useful substances different foods contain, and in what quantities. These useful substances are called nutrients.

Scientists who work for the British Ministry of Agriculture & Fisheries have found that a small tin of baked beans (225 grams) contains:

144 KILOCALORIES OF ENERGY
11.5 GRAMS OF PROTEIN
1.1 GRAMS OF FAT
23.2 GRAMS OF CARBOHYDRATE
0.1 GRAMS OF CALCIUM
3.1 MILLIGRAMS OF IRON
0.1 MILLIGRAMS OF VITAMIN A
0.2 MILLIGRAMS OF THIAMIN
0.1 MILLIGRAMS OF RIBOFLAVIN
2.9 MILLIGRAMS OF NICOTINIC ACID
NO VITAMIN C
NO VITAMIN D
166.5 GRAMS OF WATER

AMAZING!

The names of the chemicals on this list may be completely meaningless to most people, but our bodies know exactly what to do with them. We don't even have to think about it.

Scientists only began to understand how different sorts of food are used by the body once they found out that food, our bodies, and indeed everything is made of tiny parts called molecules.

Molecules

A molecule is the smallest piece of a substance you can possibly have – and that is incredibly small. A bowl of sugar contains hundreds and thousands of tiny pieces of sugar. If you broke one of those pieces in half, you'd still have sugar. If it were possible to break it in half again and again, it would still be sugar until finally the pieces would be the size of molecules. If you broke apart the molecules, you wouldn't have sugar any more.

Each grain of sugar contains about 1,000,000,000,000,000,000 molecules. That many *grains* of sugar would cover twenty four football fields right up to the top of the goal posts.

Molecules are so amazingly small that scientists can't see them, even with the most powerful microscopes. The only way to learn about them is to study large groups of molecules. We know that large groups of sugar molecules form into white crystals, dissolve in water and taste sweet. Salt is made of groups of salt molecules. A glass of water is a group of water molecules.

A substance made of a group of one sort of molecule is called a chemical. The chemicals called sugar, salt, and water look, feel and taste different because their molecules are different.

As you can see from the list of ingredients on a baked beans tin (see page 8), most food is a mixture of different chemicals. As soon as you eat some food, your body begins to sort out the chemicals.

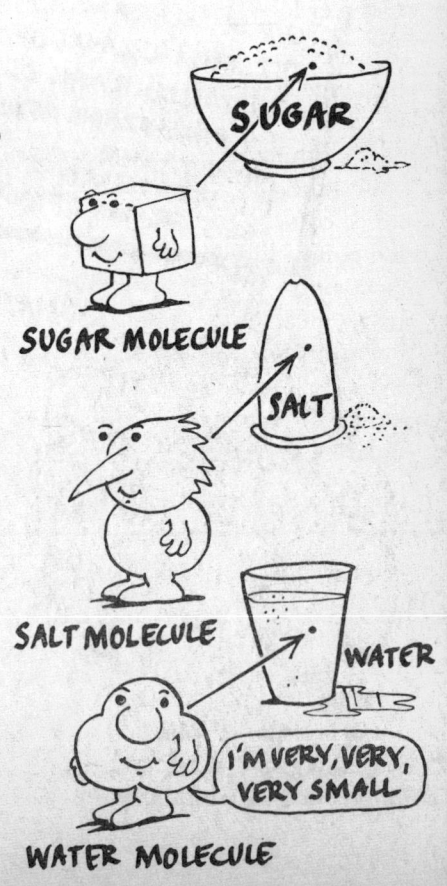

Digestion

The poet Walter De La Mare wrote:

It's a very odd thing
As odd as can be
That whatever Miss T eats,
Turns into Miss T.

It does seem odd that no matter what sort of food we eat, we still grow in the same way. A chicken dinner doesn't make us feel more like a chicken! No matter how many crisps we eat, we never look like a crisp.

This is because our food starts to change as soon as it enters the mouth. After a few hours it looks nothing like the food that was on the plate. If you are like most people, you have been sick quite a few times and know only too well how unlike food a meal looks and tastes a few hours after it has been eaten. This change takes place as the food travels through the digestive system.

The digestive system is a long tube like a hosepipe, with a bulge called the stomach. It takes the food on a long and bendy journey from the mouth to the anus. In adults, the digestive system is usually over five metres long. You can often hear a gurgling sound as the food is squeezed along the tube.

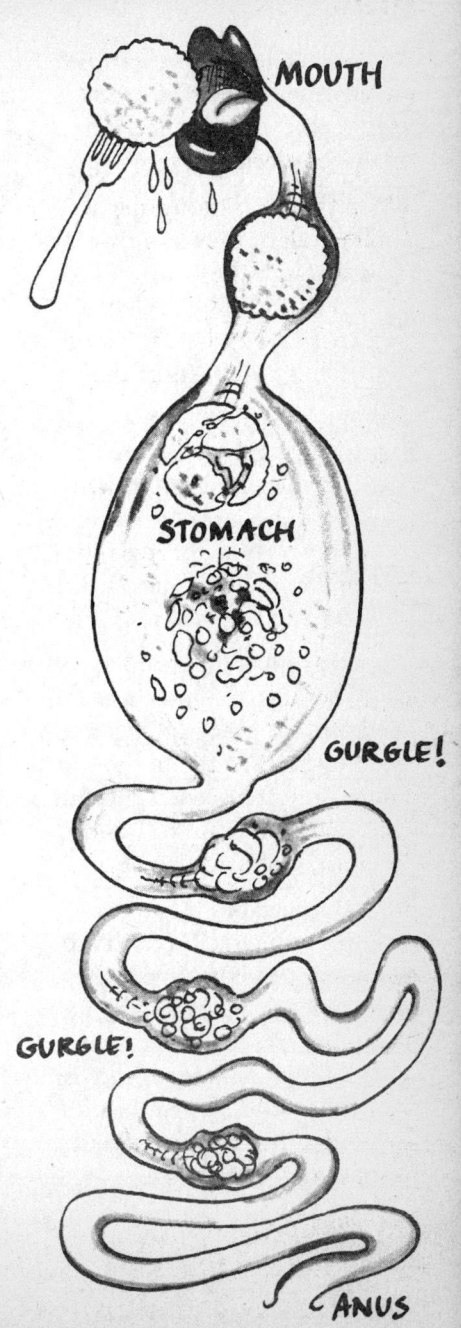

Inside the tube, there are special body chemicals called digestive enzymes. These enzymes make the large molecules of food break apart into smaller and smaller molecules.

When the food molecules are small enough, they can travel right through the walls of the digestive tube. The molecules are carried away by the blood and taken to all parts of the body.

Some of the molecules that are in the food cannot be broken apart by the digestive enzymes. They travel right through the tube and come out again a day or so later in the faeces.

The small molecules which leave the digestive tube are a bit like building blocks. They are taken to parts of the body where they are needed and put back together again to build different, larger molecules.

So, the molecules that were once part of Miss T's food are taken apart by her digestive system and put together again to replace bits that have been worn out, or damaged. If Miss T is still a child, the molecules are used as building materials so she can grow.

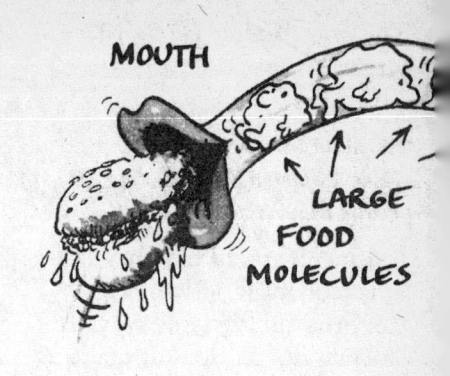

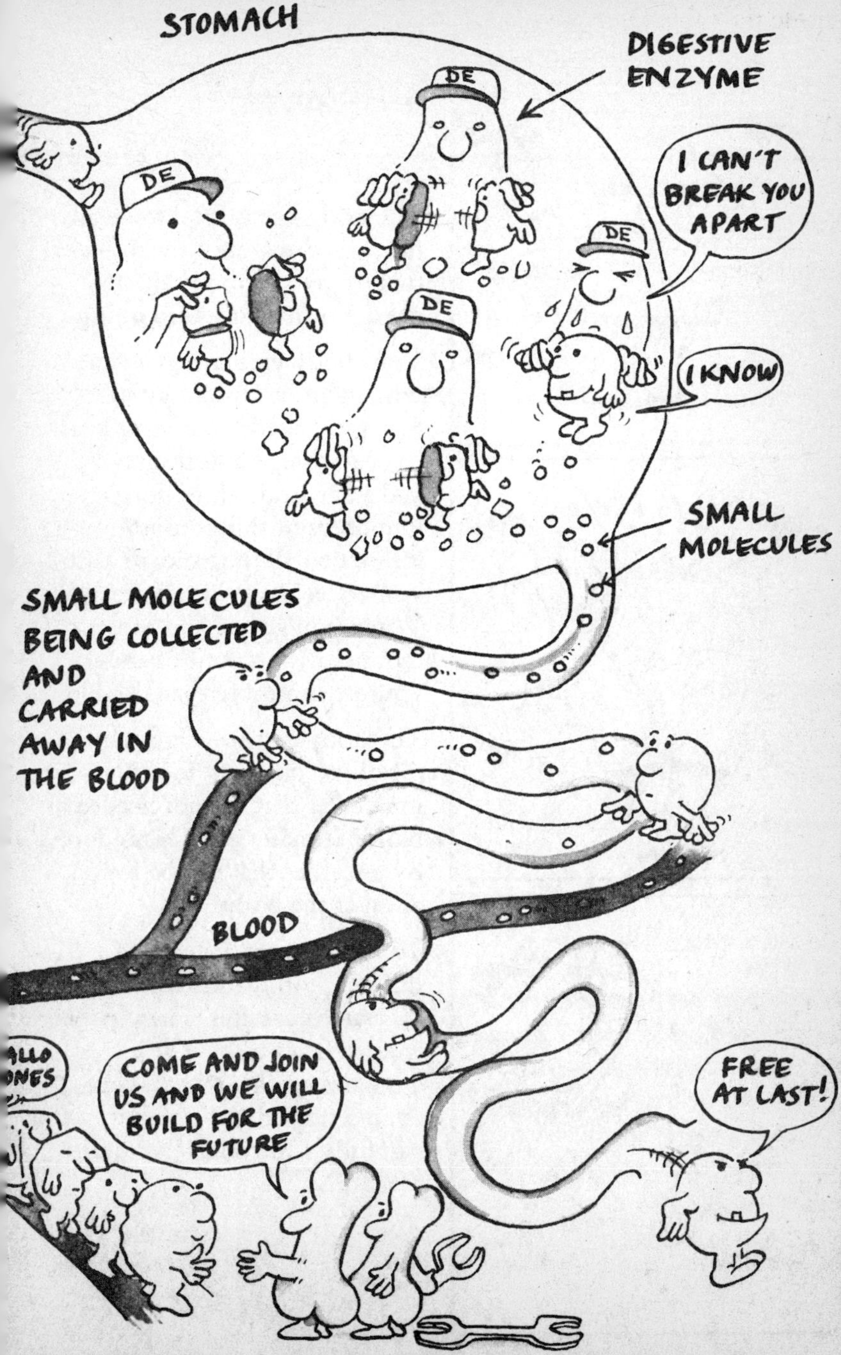
STOMACH
DIGESTIVE ENZYME
DE
I CAN'T BREAK YOU APART
I KNOW
SMALL MOLECULES
SMALL MOLECULES BEING COLLECTED AND CARRIED AWAY IN THE BLOOD
BLOOD
COME AND JOIN US AND WE WILL BUILD FOR THE FUTURE
FREE AT LAST!

Getting energy from food

The body needs food molecules for something else as well – as a fuel to give the body the energy it needs to keep going.

Your body uses energy even when you lie absolutely still. Energy is needed for your heart to beat, your lungs to breathe and your stomach to gurgle. Hundreds of things must go on inside you all the time, to keep you alive. They all take energy. When you get up and move around, the amount of energy you use can more than double.

The body gets its energy by carefully 'burning' food molecules that are not needed as building materials. This is done by enzymes that can be found all over the body.

These enzymes have quite a different job than that of digestive enzymes. They gather energy from food. The enzymes do this by breaking apart the food molecules in carefully controlled chemical reactions.

A chemical reaction is something that turns one substance into another substance. For example, a car getting rusty is a chemical reaction. The metal of the car is turning to rust.

If you want to see a chemical reaction that takes place more quickly than this, mix some bicarbonate of soda with vinegar. (If you don't have them at home, they can be bought in a food shop.)

The mixture will go fizzy almost immediately. As molecules of bicarbonate of soda touch molecules in the vinegar, they break apart. Parts of the bicarbonate of soda molecules join with parts of the molecules in vinegar. New molecules are made. One of these is carbon dioxide, the gas that is found in fizzy drinks. (Don't drink your mixture, it will taste horrible!)

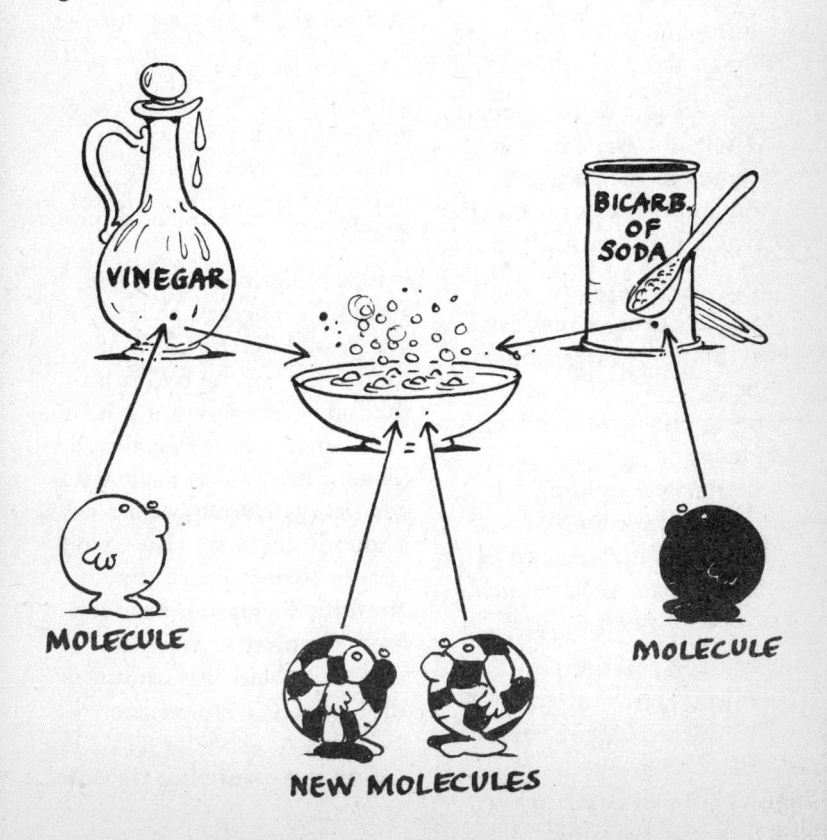

VINEGAR

BICARB. OF SODA

MOLECULE

NEW MOLECULES

MOLECULE

If you light a candle, you are starting a chemical reaction. As the candle burns, candle wax and oxygen from the air are turning into carbon dioxide and water.

You can't see the oxygen and carbon dioxide because they are invisible gases. But if you place a glass jar over the burning candle, two things will happen:

1 The candle will soon go out. This is because the jar stops any more oxygen from getting to the flame – the place where the reaction is taking place.

2 Water and soot will collect on the walls of the jar. The water was formed in the chemical reaction and the soot is candle wax which hasn't completely reacted.

As a candle burns, it releases carbon dioxide, water, and soot into the air. But it releases something else as well – energy in the form of light and heat. This energy was holding together the molecules of candle wax. When molecules are broken apart in a chemical reaction, energy can escape.

The chemical reactions in the body break apart molecules of food in much the same way. The difference is, the body doesn't allow all the energy stored in food to escape.

Special enzymes break apart the food molecules bit by bit. As this happens, oxygen from the air (which we take in when we breathe) reacts with the food to make carbon dioxide and water.

We breathe out the carbon dioxide. The water joins the rest of the water in the body, and as much of the energy as possible is captured by the bodies own molecules. This energy will be used to keep the body going.

Some of the energy can't be captured. It is released as heat, and helps to keep us warm. That is why you feel warm if you run hard and use a lot of energy.

It is possible to measure the amount of energy the body can get from different kinds of food. This is done by burning the food and finding out how much energy is released in the form of heat. Obviously this is not always as straightforward as it sounds. How do you burn a glass of orange juice? But by carefully drying out the food and burning it in insulated containers, scientists can work out how much stored energy each type of food contains. The energy is measured in Calories.

Counting Calories

You may have heard people talking about counting Calories and worrying that some of the food which they eat contains too many Calories.

A calorie is the amount of heat it takes to raise the temperature of one millilitre of water by one degree centigrade. When people say 'Calorie', they actually mean 'kilocalorie', which is one thousand calories. But since kilocalorie is a bit of a mouthful, many people say 'Calorie' but spell it with a capital 'C' so everyone will know they mean kilocalorie.

If you look back to page 9 you will see that the small tin of baked beans was found to contain 144 kilocalories (Calories). Scientists have found that a glass of milk contains about 126 Calories, an apple 60, and a bar of chocolate about 350.

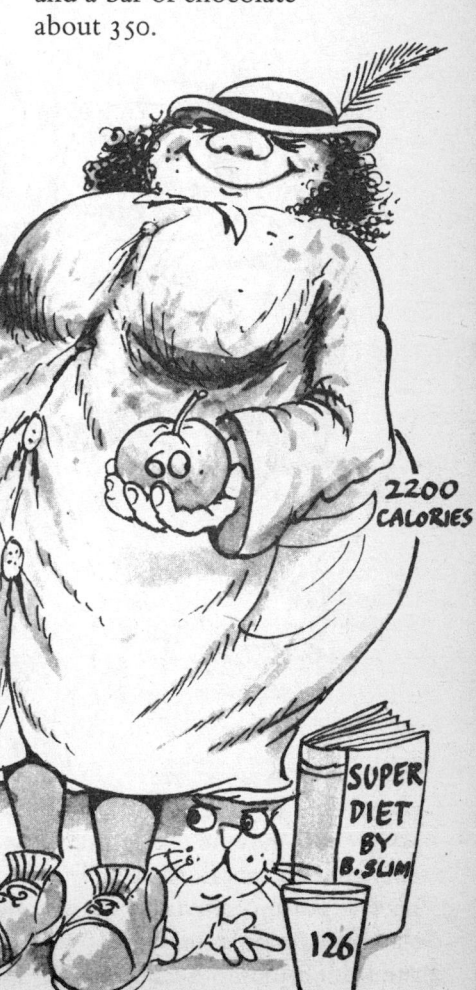

The amount of Calories which your body uses depends on several things. The more exercise you take, the more energy you need – just as a car needs more fuel the more it is driven. The bigger your body is, the more energy it uses – just as a large car needs more fuel than a small one.

If you are growing or recovering from an injury, your body may be using more energy than usual so you will need to eat more. And it seems that some people just need more food than others – no-one knows why.

In some parts of the world almost everyone has more food than they need. They eat food which they enjoy even when they're not hungry. This means that they probably take in more Calories than they need, so they have plenty of extra energy to play sports.

Some scientists believe that certain people have so much extra energy that their bodies get rid of it by wasting it – 'burning' it off as heat.

If your body doesn't use all the Calories you eat, it will use the extra energy to put together molecules of fat. The fat will be stored in your body. Later on, your body might need more energy than you are getting from your food. Then, the molecules of fat are broken apart again to release the energy.

Everyone who has enough to eat has some fat stored in their body – even if they look very thin. It's only sensible to put some fat away in case of hard times. But many people feel that they have too much fat. That is why they count Calories.

Small children need fewer Calories than adults because their bodies are smaller. But once a person reaches the age of 8 or 9, they will need to eat almost as many Calories as a medium sized adult. This is about 2,000 to 2,500 Calories a day. Large men who get a lot of exercise can burn up more than 3,500 Calories a day.

Let's say you use 2,200 Calories a day. You could get that energy by eating 15.3 small tins of baked beans at 144 Calories each. Or you could eat 36.67 apples at 60 Calories each, or 6.29 chocolate bars at 350 Calories each. But if you did, you wouldn't be very healthy. In fact, you would eventually die because energy is only one of the things you need from food.

WE NEED SOME MORE ENERGY

ENERGY

2200 CALORIES

2200 CALORIES

2200 CALORIES

The molecules building the body

The body also uses molecules from food as building materials. New molecules need to be made as the body grows, or to replace bits that have worn out.

Do you remember how many molecules there are in a grain of sugar? The human body is about a hundred thousand million times the size of a grain of sugar, so you can imagine how many molecules it contains!

The reason why the living body can move and think and feel is that its molecules are all working together.

The body is made up of thousands of different kinds of molecules. Most of them are grouped together to make cells. The cells are grouped together to make organs (like the heart and liver) or tissues (like muscles and skin). The organs and tissues are grouped together to make the whole body.

The body works because there are millions of chemical reactions going on inside it all the time. Almost all these reactions are triggered and carefully controlled by the body molecules called enzymes.

You know that there are special enzymes, in the digestive tube. Thousands of other enzymes in the body do all sorts of different jobs.

Other sorts of molecules in the blood, can identify and destroy invading bacteria and viruses. There are molecules that carry oxygen, food, waste and even messages around the body.

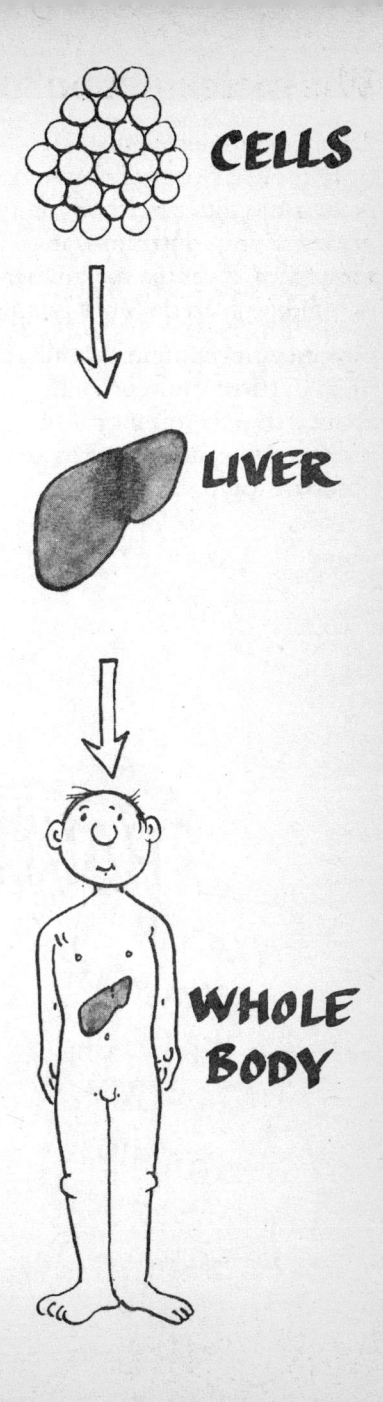

CELLS

↓

LIVER

↓

WHOLE BODY

What makes food nutritious?

Each food molecule that is carried out of your digestive system and into your body is good for you (nutritious) in some way. It can be used either as building material or as fuel.

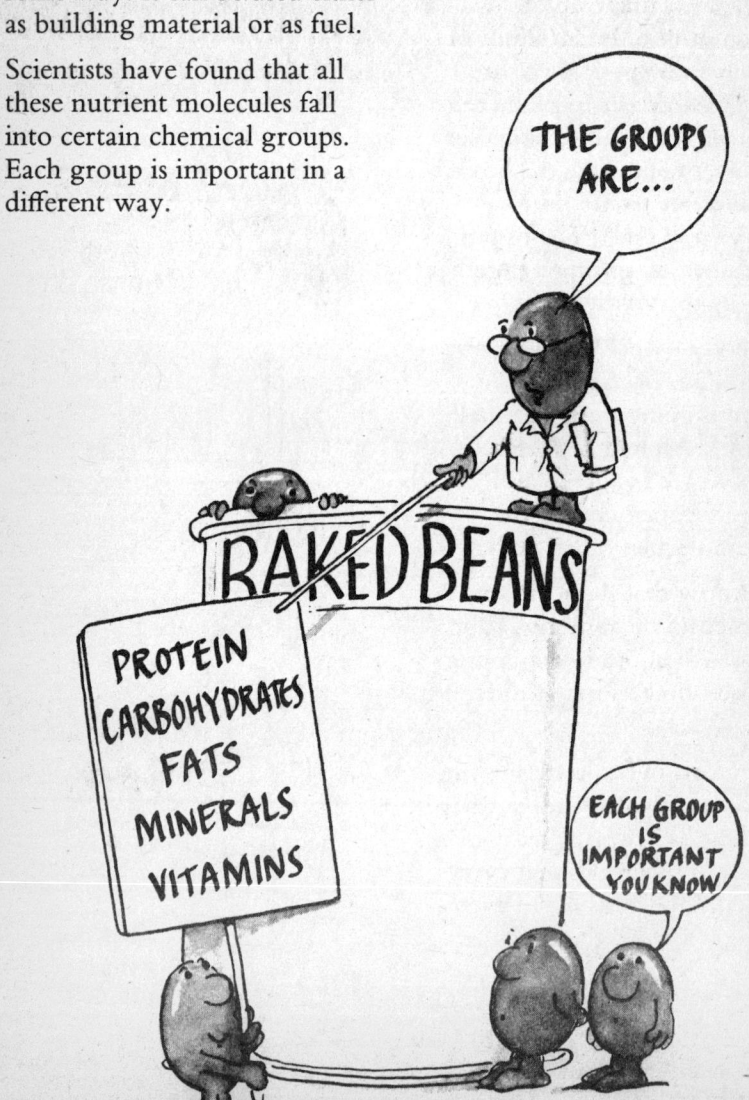

Scientists have found that all these nutrient molecules fall into certain chemical groups. Each group is important in a different way.

THE GROUPS ARE...

PROTEIN
CARBOHYDRATES
FATS
MINERALS
VITAMINS

EACH GROUP IS IMPORTANT YOU KNOW

Protein

It is absolutely necessary to eat food that contains protein. The human body, like the bodies of all animals, is made mostly of protein.

Protein molecules come in billions of different shapes and sizes. They do most of the important complicated jobs in the body: fighting viruses, carrying oxygen, extracting energy from food, making the muscles move and thousands of other things.

The body is always repairing itself and replacing these molecules, so it needs new supplies of protein from food.

It's impossible to work out exactly how much protein a person needs. Generally, the bigger a person is, the more protein he needs. A person who is growing or recovering from an injury or illness needs extra protein.

If you weigh between 40 and 50 kilograms you ought to eat at least 40 grams of protein a day.

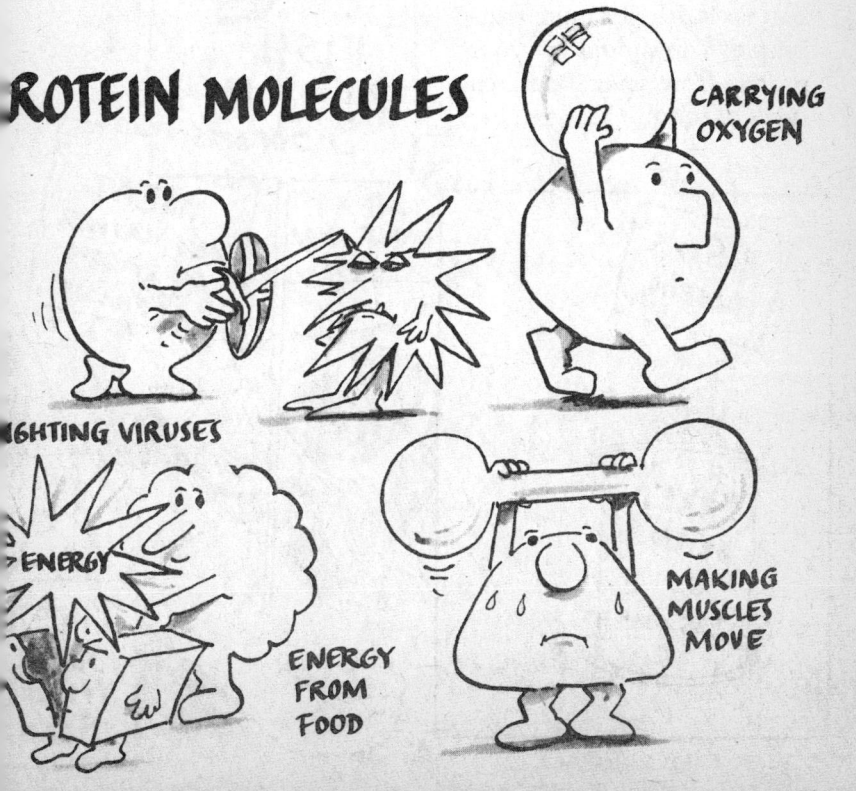

PROTEIN MOLECULES

CARRYING OXYGEN

FIGHTING VIRUSES

ENERGY FROM FOOD

MAKING MUSCLES MOVE

It is important to eat regular supplies of protein because your body isn't able to store it for later. If you eat more than enough protein on Monday, the extra will be broken down for energy. You'll still have to eat your full supply of protein on Tuesday.

Many different foods contain protein. So it isn't very difficult to get a regular supply. The 225g tin of baked beans (see page 9) was found to contain 11.5g of protein. This doesn't mean that 6 tins of baked beans will give you all the protein you need. It's not quite that simple. You should get your protein from several different types of food.

MEAT
SAUSAGE
6 GRAMS

FISH
ONE FISH FINGER
3.5 GRAMS

MEAT
LAMB CHOP
12 GMS.

MEAT
ONE RASHER
OF BACON
7 GRAMS

11.5 GMS.
PROTEIN

BAKED BEANS
225 GMS.

CHEESE
SMALL
PIECE
8 GMS.

The largest supplies of protein are found in: meat, chicken, fish, nuts, cheese, eggs, milk, ice cream.

Fruits and leafy vegetables contain very little protein, although they are full of many other useful molecules.

Sugar, boiled sweets and mints contain no protein at all. They are really only good for providing energy. (They're high in Calories.)

Almost all other sorts of food contain some protein. As long as you eat enough different kinds of food, you'll get plenty of protein.

MILK ONE GLASS 6 GRAMS

ICE CREAM TWO SCOOPS 8 GRAMS

BREAD ONE SLICE 2 GRAMS

EGGS ONE MEDIUM EGG 7 GRAMS

NUTS ONE 50 GRAM PACKET OF PEANUTS 12 GRAMS

CHICKEN ONE LEG 12 GRAMS

What makes protein?

Different sorts of food which contain protein don't all look and taste the same. A sausage tastes very different from an egg, for instance. There are two reasons for this:

1 The protein molecules are mixed up with other molecules which also help to give the food its taste, appearance and texture.

2 There are many, different sorts of protein molecules. Hair and fingernails are made mostly of protein; so is the white of an egg. Protein molecules can feel different, look different, and do different jobs. But they are all built in much the same way – whether they're in a sausage or in you.

Imagine a long string of beads all tangled up in a ball. A protein molecule is rather like that. The 'beads' are smaller molecules, called amino acids. They are bonded together end to end to make a chain.

There are 20 different sorts of amino acids. They can be arranged along the chain in millions of different ways. Each different arrangement will make a different kind of protein molecule. A protein molecule can have over a thousand amino acids in the chain.

This is why there are so many different types of protein molecules – both in our own bodies and in those of every other living creature.

PROTEIN MOLECULE

AMINO ACID

AMINO ACID

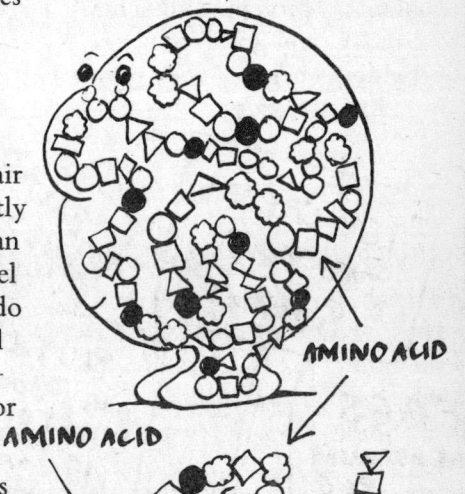

DIFFERENT COMBINATIONS OF 5 AMINO ACIDS

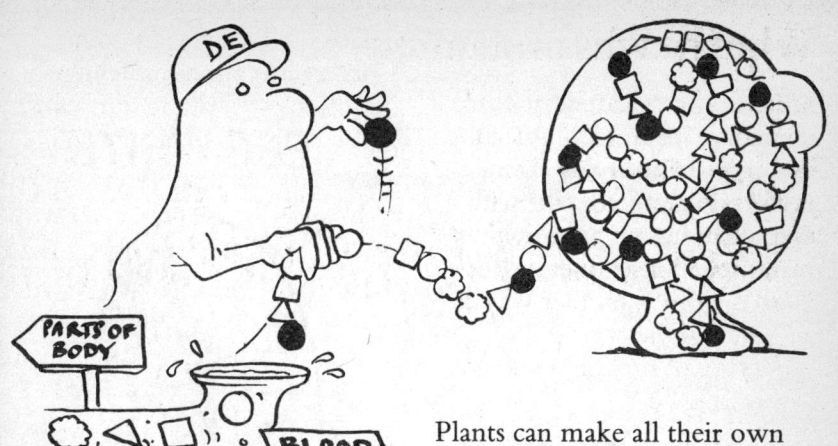

When you eat protein, it is broken down into its individual amino acids while it travels through the digestive tube.

The amino acids are absorbed by the blood and carried round the body. They are taken to wherever protein is needed in the body. Then they are put together in a combination that is distinctly human; and may be distinctly you.

The body can make 12 of the 20 amino acids it needs to build protein. We have to eat protein to get supplies of the other eight amino acids.

Plants can make all their own amino acids. So can many micro-organisms, like yeast and bacteria. Cows and many other grass-eating animals don't have to eat protein. They have large numbers of bacteria living inside them which make amino acids. These amino acids are used by the animals.

Animals are made of the same sort of amino acids as we are. So eating protein from animals (meat, fish, eggs or milk) will give us all the amino acids we need. Plants are rather different. Their protein may contain very little of one or two of the essential amino acids.

This doesn't mean we have to eat animal protein in order to get all the amino acids we need. Scientists have found that amino acids which are low in one sort of plant are plentiful in other sorts. That's why it's best to eat as many different plant foods as you can.

Take the white of an egg

Scientists have learned about the nature of protein molecules by carefully purifying them, performing experiments with them, and testing them with complicated instruments. But there is a much simpler way to see some of the chemical properties of protein; look at an egg white.

An egg white is one eighth protein. The other seven eighths is mostly water, so it's one of the purest solutions of protein that can be found in nature. There are 5 main types of protein molecules in an egg white.

You may have noticed that a raw egg white seems to cling together in a glob and forms long sticky strings when you try to separate it. This is because there are huge protein molecules in egg white that are wrapped around one another. Egg white is literally a tangle of protein molecules.

Like most protein molecules, those in egg white are very delicate. The long chain of amino acids is tangled up to make a precise shape.

The shape of many protein molecules can alter very easily. If you want to see this happen, put an egg white in boiling water or on a hot frying pan. It will go hard almost at once. This is because most of the protein molecules in the egg white turn solid. The same sort of thing happens to the protein in meat or fish when it is cooked.

Try mixing an acid, like lemon juice or vinegar, with an egg white. The egg white will turn hard. This is because a change of acidity will make protein molecules change shape. The same thing happens if you add one of these acids to milk. Hard bits of protein form and float around in the milk.

The proteins in an egg white are so delicate, even physically damaging them will turn the protein slightly solid. This is what happens when egg whites are beaten into a foam with a whisk.

The chemical characteristics of protein in egg white can be useful. Cooks use them to make meringues. If you want to try to make meringues you'll need:

1 *At least one egg white, separated from its yolk. (Be careful not to allow the yolk to burst during the separation. Chemicals in the yolk will interfere with the chemicals needed to make meringues.)*
2 *½ a teaspoon of lemon juice or vinegar for each egg white.*
3 *4 tablespoons of sugar for each egg white.*
4 *An oven set at 120°C (250°F gas mark 1).*

Let the egg white stand for half an hour, until it is the same temperature as the room.

Froth up the egg white with a whisk until it is a light foam. Then add the acid (lemon juice or vinegar). This will help to harden the protein and make a firmer foam. Keep whisking as you gradually add the sugar.

When the foam stands up in peaks, it is ready for the oven. By then, your arm might be quite tired.

Spoon the foam onto a greased baking tin and put it in the oven. After three hours in the oven, the heat will have made the egg white protein hard. Your meringue will be ready to eat!

Carbohydrates

Carbohydrate is not an essential part of our diet the way protein is. The human body does not need carbohydrate molecules as building blocks for growing and repairing itself. But carbohydrate is important for us and most other animals on earth. It is our main source of energy from food.

Carbohydrate molecules attached together in different ways can make hundreds of different things. Wood is mostly carbohydrate and so are cotton clothes. The paper that makes up the pages of this book and food like sugar, fruit, vegetables and bread are also made mostly of carbohydrate molecules. What do all these things have in common? They are all made from plants.

The carbohydrate manufacturing plant

The bodies of animals are built mainly from protein. But plants are built mainly from carbohydrates. Plants don't have to eat to get the building materials they need to grow. They can make their own carbohydrates.

Plants use energy from sunlight to bond together molecules of carbon dioxide from the air and molecules of water. This makes larger molecules, called simple sugars.

Simple sugars are carbohydrates. They are the basic building blocks from which most of the plant is made.

Simple sugars are found in many foods, such as honey, fruit and sweets. When we eat simple sugars, they can be broken down by the body and their stored energy is released for us to use (see page 14).

The sugar that we put in tea, or on cereal, is actually two simple sugars joined together. Table sugar comes from two kinds of plants, sugar cane and sugar beet. These plants store the simple sugars they have made in the form of a double molecule.

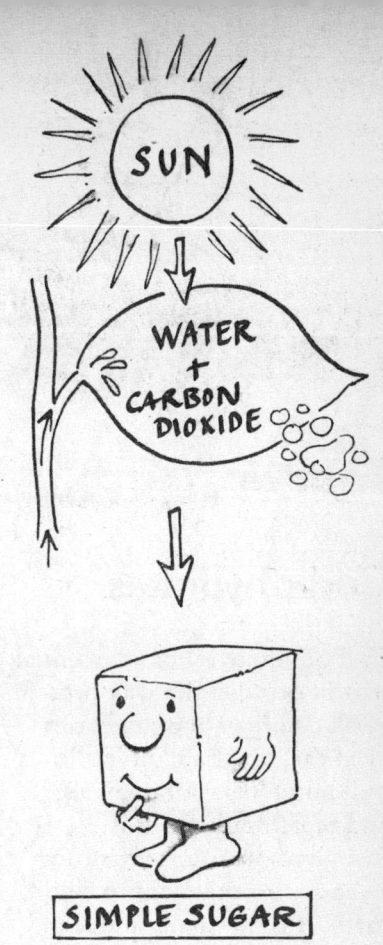

When we eat table sugar, this double molecule is broken down by chemicals in our digestive system. It is broken into two simple sugars. These sugars can then be absorbed by the body and used for energy.

Just as our body can only use protein in the form of individual amino acids, it can only use carbohydrates which are in the form of simple sugars.

Carbohydrate that isn't food

Most of the simple sugar molecules made by plants are bonded together to make long chains. These chains of simple sugars are called cellulose. Cellulose is quite unlike sugar. It does not taste the slightest bit sweet and will not dissolve in water.

The cellulose chains in plants are bundled together into tough fibres. These are the plants' main building materials. It is cellulose that holds a plant's stem rigid, makes carrots crunch, and gives fruit its tough protective skin. Cellulose is the main ingredient in wood, paper and cotton.

Have you ever wondered why horses and cows can eat grass and we can't? It's because grass is mainly made from cellulose. Our bodies can't digest this. It has to do with the special way in which the simple sugar molecules are joined together to make cellulose. The chemicals in our stomach and small intestine simply cannot break the molecules apart.

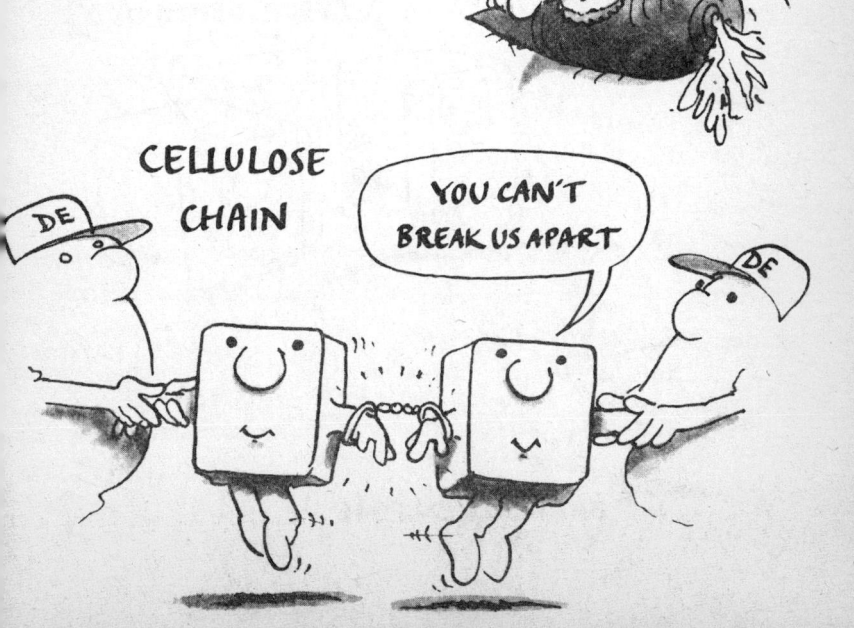

Cellulose always passes right through our digestive system and out in the faeces. This is why grass is not nutritious for humans – nor is cotton wool, paper or sawdust.

Animals that live on grass are able to digest cellulose. Their digestive system has an extra organ where millions of bacteria live. These bacteria have enzymes that can break the bonds in the cellulose and release the simple sugars. Some of these sugars are used by the bacteria and the rest are used by the animal.

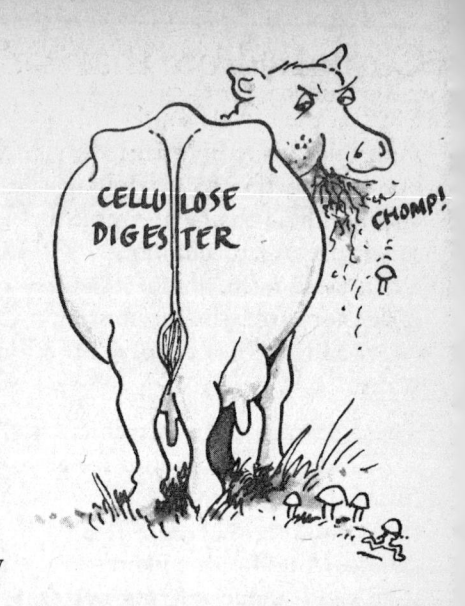

STARCH CHAIN

Carbohydrate that is food

Plants don't only make simple sugars into cellulose. If that were true, no plants would be useful food for us.

Plants can also link simple sugars into a different kind of chain, called starch. The bonds in this chain *can* be broken by our digestive system. The starch chain is not strong enough to be useful as a building material for plants. It is made as a way of storing simple sugars.

Most plants have a place where they store starch. Carrot and turnip plants store it in their roots over the winter. They use the starch as food when the plants start to grow in spring.

Potato plants have special storage organs that grow just underground (the potatoes). Wheat and beans store starch in their seeds. When new plants grow from the seeds, they will have a good supply of food in their first few weeks of life.

The place where starch is stored is the most nutritious part of the plant. It is the part we usually eat. We eat the roots of carrots and turnips, the storage organs of potato plants and the seeds of beans and wheat.

How to find starch

You can find out where a plant stores its starch by doing a simple chemical test. Iodine is a chemical that reacts with starch. It makes the starch, which is usually white or colourless, turn dark blue.

Iodine dissolved in water can be bought at a chemist. It is a red brown liquid used to disinfect cuts.

Pour a few tablespoons of the iodine solution into a small shallow dish. It should just cover the bottom. Place a slice of carrot, or potato (or any piece of plant you want to test) in the dish. Leave it for a few minutes. Wash the plant sample and look for the blue part. That is where the starch is.
IMPORTANT: Do *not* eat the plant sample after testing it.
IODINE IS POISONOUS.

If you test flour with your iodine, you will find it contains lots of starch. Flour is the ground up seeds of wheat. The seeds contain a large store of starch, and some protein, for the young wheat plant when it begins to grow.

Many different types of food are made with flour. Bread, cakes and spaghetti are three examples. They will all react very strongly with iodine. Try it.

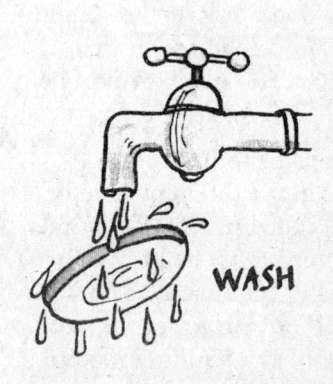

The iodine test can also be used to show the work of a digestive enzyme. In saliva, there is a digestive enzyme which reacts with starch. The enzyme breaks up starch into simple sugars.

Iodine will only react with simple sugars that are linked together in large starch molecules. Once starch has reacted with saliva it should no longer react with iodine to become dark blue.

You can try this experiment with your own saliva and any sample of starch. Try using a potato. Take a thin slice, cover one side of it with saliva and leave it for at least ten minutes (the longer the better). Then do the iodine test.

The side that has been treated with saliva may still turn slightly blue. It is unlikely that all the starch will react with the enzyme in saliva. But it should be a much paler blue than the side which wasn't covered with saliva.

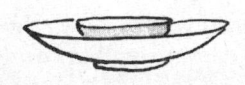

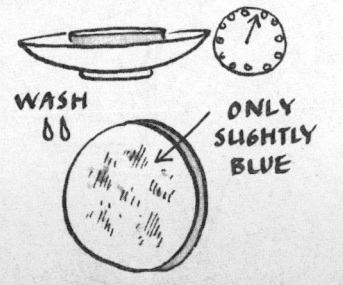

LEAVE 10 MINS.

LEAVE FOR A FEW MINUTES

WASH

ONLY SLIGHTLY BLUE

BAKED BEAN DOING THE SALIVA TEST

Cooking carbohydrates

Carbohydrates are part of every meal you eat. All food except fats, eggs, meat, fish and some types of cheese contains carbohydrate. Almost every recipe has carbohydrate of some sort in the list of ingredients.

The tin of baked beans which you read about on page 9 has 23.2 grams of carbohydrate. It contains over twice as much carbohydrate as protein. Some of this is starch that was stored in the beans. (They are the seeds of the bean plant.)

The list of ingredients on the tin shows that two other types of carbohydrate were added when the beans were cooked in the factory. These were sugar and foodstarch.

Sugar was added to make the beans taste sweeter. The starch was added to make the beans look and feel nicer to eat.

For many years, cooks have been taking advantage of a very interesting characteristic of starch. Plants store their starch in tiny packets, called granules. The packets are so small that they can only be seen with a microscope. These granules will not dissolve in water.

Try adding a spoonful of flour or cornstarch to a cup of cold water. You will see that the powder does not dissolve and disappear the way sugar or salt would. But if you put the water and starch mixture in a saucepan and heat it, an interesting change will occur.

Stir the mixture as you heat it. As the water gets hotter it seeps inside the starch granules, making them grow bigger and bigger. As this happens, the water will become thicker and more syrupy. The more starch you add in the beginning, the thicker the liquid will become.

RICE

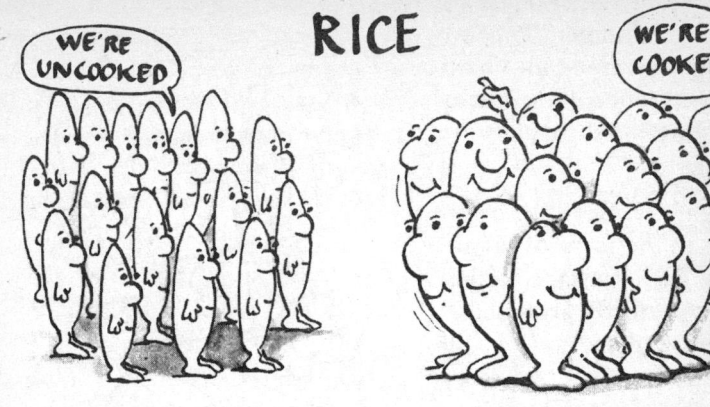

The same thing happens if you use other liquids like milk, fruit juice or gravy instead of water. Starch is used to thicken soup, most types of custard – and the sauce in baked beans.

Have you ever noticed what happens to rice and spaghetti when they are boiled? Rice or spaghetti which comes in packets is hard. But when they are put in water and boiled they become softer. As they become softer, each grain of rice or piece of spaghetti gets larger.

This is because rice and spaghetti contain starch granules. The granules soak up the hot water, like a sponge does. They swell up and get softer. If you want to see how much water they soak up, weigh a portion of rice or spaghetti before and after boiling.

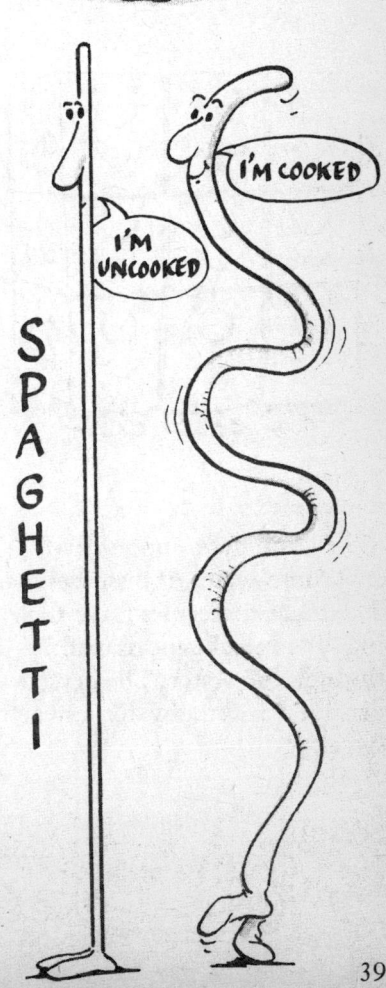

Boiling water can also change ordinary table sugar. This is how sugar is turned into hard sweets and toffee. It's done by rearranging the sugar molecules.

The sugar we use in tea or on cereal is in the form of sugar crystals. Each crystal contains stacks of perfectly arranged sugar molecules.

More sugar molecules will dissolve in hot water than cold. This is because making the water warmer makes the molecules begin to move more and more quickly.

When you put a spoonful of sugar into water, it dissolves. The sugar molecules leave their organised stacks and spread through the water. The crystals disappear and the water tastes sweet.

Sweets are made by dissolving a large amount of sugar in quite a small amount of very hot water. This can be done on an ordinary stove but BE CAREFUL. Don't do it unless there is an experienced cook around to help.

Put three or four tablespoons of sugar in a small saucepan and add a cup of water. Heat the water on top of the stove and stir. It's best to use a wooden spoon which won't absorb heat from the hot sugar mixture.

As the water gets warmer, all the sugar will dissolve. Gradually add more sugar spoonful by spoonful and keep stirring. Once the mixture starts to boil, turn the heat down so it just bubbles gently.

Eventually you will have added so much sugar that the mixture will be thick and syrupy. It actually contains more sugar than water. But the heat of the mixture keeps the molecules moving and stops them from being rearranged into crystals.

WHAT DO YOU SUPPOSE WOULD HAPPEN IF THE HOT MIXTURE WERE SUDDENLY COOLED DOWN?

THIS! I GUESS

Put a bowl of cold water beside the stove. Pour a spoonful of the hot sugar syrup into the water. The sugar will cool down very quickly. In a few seconds it will be cool enough to touch. Reach into the water and pick it out. It should feel quite hard. If it doesn't, let the mixture boil for another minute and try again. Keep trying every minute or so and soon you will find that the spoonful of syrup goes hard and brittle when you drop it into the water.

Then pour the hot sugar syrup onto a metal baking tin. It will all go hard – like a large flat boiled-sweet. This is because the mixture cooled very suddenly, so the sugar molecules suddenly slowed down and went solid. It happened so quickly that the molecules didn't have time to reform into nice ordered crystals. Instead, they formed into a hard glob of disorganised sugar molecules.

Many of the sweets you buy in the shops are made like this. They just have flavourings and colouring added. Toffee contains butter or margarine as well as sugar. But the main ingredient in many sweets is disorganised sugar molecules.

A cookery book will tell you how to make these molecules into something that looks and tastes good.

DISORGANISED SUGAR MOLECULES LEMON FLAVOUR

Eating carbohydrates

Sugar and starch are very important in the human diet as a source of energy. But they are not body building molecules, like protein, so we don't *need* to eat them.

Some food scientists believe that cellulose may be the most important carbohydrate for us to eat, even though it is not absorbed by the body.

The more common names for cellulose are 'roughage' or 'fibre'. It is well known as a substance that cures or prevents constipation by helping the digestive system form faeces. The undigested cellulose molecules make the faeces softer and bulkier. This means that it's easier for the muscles in the digestive tube to push the faeces along.

Scientists have found that people who eat foods containing lots of cellulose (such as fresh fruits and vegetables and brown bread) are often healthier than people who eat more sweet, starchy or fatty foods.

The scientists still don't know why this is true. But many people have started to eat brown bread instead of white bread and are eating more fruit and vegetables instead of cakes and sweets.

How much sugar do you eat in a day? Think about all the sweet things you eat, as well as sugar on cereal or in drinks.

Human beings ate very few sweet foods until about 150 years ago. Then, we learned how to extract sugar from sugar cane. Today, the people of Britain eat 5,800 tonnes of sugar each day. This means $4\frac{1}{2}$ tablespoons of sugar every day for each person.

Some scientists believe that this much sugar is bad for you. They have found that older people who have eaten lots of sugar during their lives seem to be more likely to have certain diseases.

Everyone knows that eating lots of sugar is bad for your teeth. Sugar sticks to your teeth and serves as food for bacteria that live in your mouth. Unless you brush the sugar and bacteria away twice a day, your teeth will start to decay.

Fat

The food you eat contains several different kinds of fat. There is the fat on meat, like pork fat or bacon fat. This can be separated from meat and concentrated to make lard. Lard is almost pure fat.

There is also fat in milk. This often separates from the rest of the milk and becomes concentrated in cream. When cream is concentrated even more, it makes butter. Like lard, butter is almost pure fat.

Some plants also contain fat. The fat is mostly found in their seeds. It can be concentrated to make margarine or cooking oil.

All fats feel slippery or greasy, but there are some differences between them. Plant fats are usually a liquid oil at room temperature. Animal fats are solid until they are warmed up.

Each type of fat is a mixture of molecules. There are many different kinds of fatty molecules in food. But all kinds of fat behave in much the same way when they are mixed with water.

You can easily see this for yourself. Half fill a jar with water. Add a spoonful of cooking oil. The oil immediately separates from the water and floats to the top. All fats do this. They are lighter than water (that is why they float) and none of them will mix with water. Scientists call fat 'hydrophobic', which is a Greek word for 'water fearing'.

Shake the liquid in the jar. The oil and water may mix for a moment, but they soon separate. The fat molecules are pushed away from the water molecules. They join together in blobs, or globules, which float to the surface.

Washing-up greasy plates would be almost impossible if people hadn't discovered a way to make fat and water mix. This is done by using soap or detergent. The molecules of these chemicals are partly water fearing (hydrophobic) and partly water loving (hydrophilic).

When a detergent like washing-up liquid is added to water, its molecules all line up in a thin film. It is these thin films that make soap bubbles. The hydrophobic ends of the detergent molecules are all on the inside of the bubbles, away from the water. The hydrophilic ends are on the outside of the bubbles, next to the water.

Add a drop of washing-up liquid to your jar of oil and water and give it a gentle shake. As they mix, the detergent molecules become sandwiched between the oil and water. The hydrophobic ends of the molecules are next to the oil and the hydrophilic ends are next to the water.

If you shake the mixture harder, the oil breaks up into tiny droplets. It doesn't separate into big globules and float to the surface any more. This is because each droplet is surrounded by a thin wall of detergent molecules that protect it from the water.

In this way, detergent makes it possible to wash away the grease in the washing-up bowl.

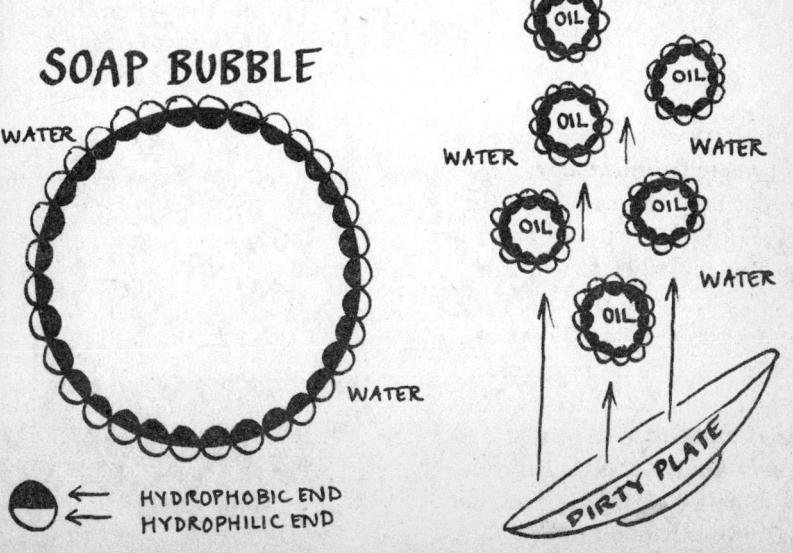

SOAP BUBBLE

WATER

WATER

← HYDROPHOBIC END
← HYDROPHILIC END

DETERGENT MOLECULE

OIL

OIL

OIL

WATER

OIL

OIL

WATER

OIL

WATER

DIRTY PLATE

The same type of molecular action makes it possible for you to digest the fat in your food. The body makes a detergent to add to the food in the digestive system. This allows the fat you've eaten to break into tiny droplets that can be absorbed by the body.

Fat molecules are used all over the body. They are part of the thin wall that surrounds each body cell. They help to make the skin and hair supple and water resistant.

Hundreds of body molecules are made from the fatty molecules found in food. But the body can also make its own fat molecules. In fact, it can make almost all the fat molecules it needs. There are some kinds of fat molecules which must be obtained from food, but they are plentiful in many kinds of food. Anyone who eats a normal mixed diet has more than enough.

Fat is the most energy rich substance in food. It is quite light, and weight for weight it holds over twice as much energy as carbohydrate.

For example:
100 grams of sugar has 394 Calories.
100 grams of cooking oil has 899 Calories.

Fat is a very convenient substance to use as an energy store. Plants mostly store energy in starch molecules. But when space is short (in some types of seeds, for instance) fat molecules are used to store energy instead.

Animals store almost all their energy in fat molecules. Unlike plants, they have to move around. They need their energy store to be as light as possible. If people got starchy when they ate too much, instead of fat, they'd be *twice* as weighty.

Minerals

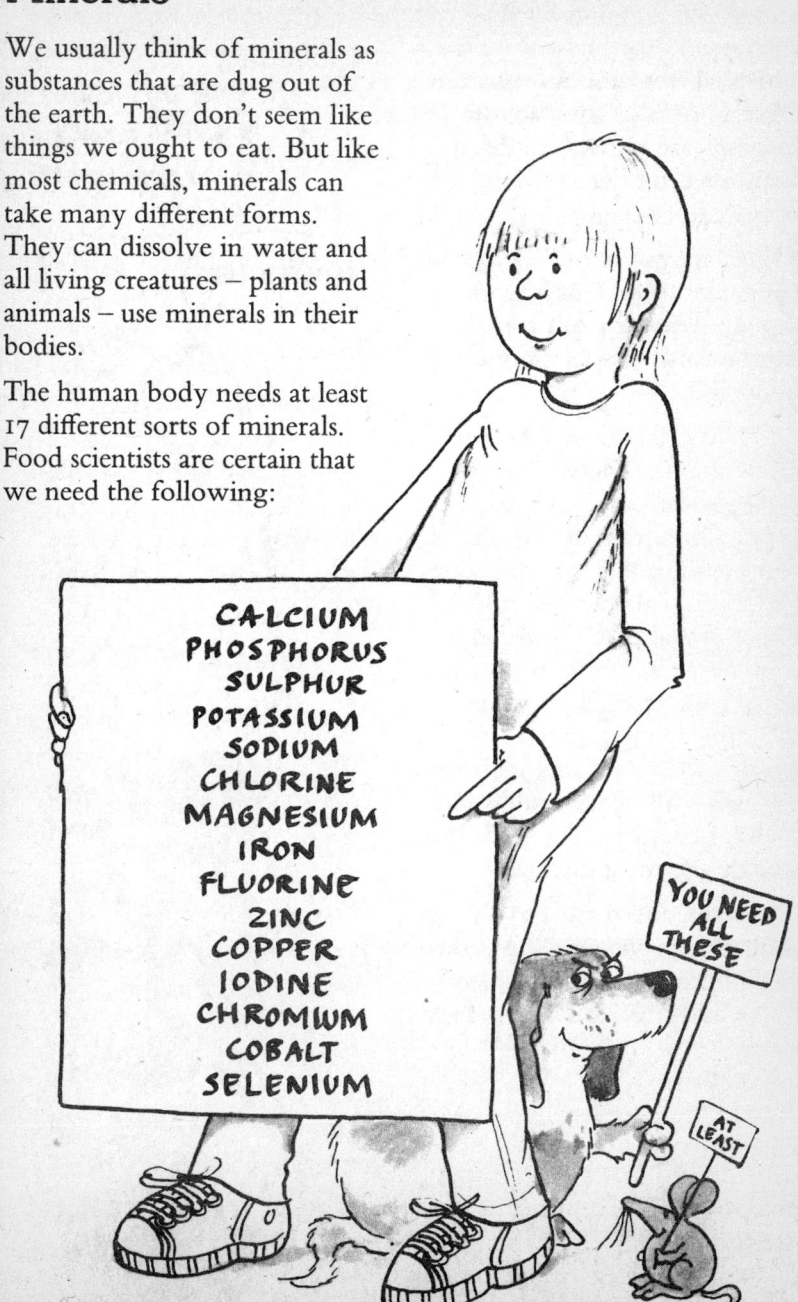

We usually think of minerals as substances that are dug out of the earth. They don't seem like things we ought to eat. But like most chemicals, minerals can take many different forms. They can dissolve in water and all living creatures – plants and animals – use minerals in their bodies.

The human body needs at least 17 different sorts of minerals. Food scientists are certain that we need the following:

- CALCIUM
- PHOSPHORUS
- SULPHUR
- POTASSIUM
- SODIUM
- CHLORINE
- MAGNESIUM
- IRON
- FLUORINE
- ZINC
- COPPER
- IODINE
- CHROMIUM
- COBALT
- SELENIUM

YOU NEED ALL THESE

AT LEAST

The minerals on the bottom part of the list are needed in very small quantities. We may also need tiny amounts of a few other minerals. If we do, the amounts are so tiny that food scientists can't detect them.

Some minerals, like copper or iodine, are poisonous if eaten in large quantities. Don't worry though. Food doesn't contain large quantities of poisonous minerals.

Calcium is the most abundant mineral in the body. The average-sized adult contains about a kilogram of calcium. Almost all of this is in the bones and teeth. Calcium and other minerals make our bones and teeth hard. It is very important to eat enough calcium when you are growing, because that is when the bones and teeth are formed. Milk, cheese and some types of bread are the foods that contain the most calcium.

The bones and teeth also contain phosphorus. This is the second most abundant mineral in the body. We each contain about $\frac{3}{4}$ of a kilogram of phosphorus.

Phosphorus is found all over the body and has many important jobs. But no one has ever been known to be ill because they weren't eating enough phosphorus. There is plenty of phosphorus in many kinds of food.

Some of the minerals are needed in quite small amounts, but that doesn't mean they aren't important. Iron is part of the red protein molecules in blood cells. It helps to capture oxygen from the air in the lungs and carry it to all parts of the body. Each blood cell lives for only a few months. When the blood cells die, the iron in them is kept and put in the new blood cells that are made.

Doctors and scientists have tried to work out how much of each sort of mineral we need to eat. We actually eat far more of most minerals than we need. The body lets many minerals pass right through the digestive system and out again in the faeces.

As long as you eat lots of different sorts of food, you'll get all the minerals you need. A small tin of baked beans (see page 9) contains 100 mg of calcium.

Food scientists believe that growing children need to eat between 500–700 mg of calcium a day. A half pint of milk will give you about 350 mg of calcium. A piece of cheese about 5 cm × 3 cm × 2 cm will give you another 300 mg of calcium. A slice of bread has about 30 mg. An orange has about 50 mg. Do you think you are getting enough calcium?

Vitamins

Years ago, many people used to get a horrible disease called scurvy. It was most common among sailors and explorers who went on long journeys. These people only ate food they could carry with them, or things they found along the way. Scurvy would make them very tired, their gums would bleed and they would bruise easily. If they didn't get medicine, they sometimes died.

There were many different medicines for scurvy: green salad, lime juice, tomatoes, oranges, pickled cabbage, small onions, green shoots from evergreen trees, horse radish, raw meat – and many more. All these medicines seemed to work but, until 1932, no-one knew why they worked.

In that year, chemists found that all these foods contained a certain substance. That substance alone would cure scurvy. We now know that humans can't survive without eating food that contains this substance. It is called vitamin C.

Scientists have found that we need to eat 13 different substances which they call vitamins:

```
VITAMIN A
THIAMIN (ALSO CALLED VITAMIN B1)
RIBOFLAVIN (ALSO CALLED VITAMIN B2)
NICOTINIC ACID
PYRIDOXINE (ALSO CALLED VITAMIN B6)
VITAMIN B12
FOLIC ACID
PANTOTHENIC ACID
BIOTIN
VITAMIN C
VITAMIN D
VITAMIN E
VITAMIN K
```

You should eat different sorts of food to make sure you get enough vitamins, just as with minerals. Some of the vitamins, such as riboflavin and vitamin B12, are mostly found in animal foods (meat, eggs and milk). Vitamin C and K are mostly found in fruits and vegetables. Vitamin A, thiamin and vitamin E are found in food from both plants and animals.

Tinned baked beans have small amounts of some vitamins. But they won't give you all the vitamins you need – even if you eat 10 tins a day. The tin of baked beans has no vitamin C or D (see page 9).

Vitamins are all molecules that work with our own body molecules. They have to be taken in as food because the body can't make them. Once inside us, vitamins aren't used up. They can be used again and again. We need only take in tiny amounts – just enough to replace any that are worn out.

One small tablet can contain all the vitamins you need to eat in a day. These tablets can be bought at the chemist, but most people get all the vitamins they need from their food.

Tinned food is sometimes low in vitamins. When food is put into tins, it is always heated to a high temperature. This is done to kill bacteria. Some vitamins, especially vitamin C, are destroyed when they get too hot. When potatoes are boiled, for instance, about half their vitamin C is destroyed.

This is why it's good for you to eat some raw food. One fresh orange will give you nearly twice as much vitamin C as you need in a whole day.

MAN MAKING VITAMIN D

Animals like cats and dogs need vitamin D as much as we do, but their fur stops sunlight from reaching their skin. They have a different way of getting vitamin D. The vitamin D chemical is pushed out of their skin and onto their fur. The sunlight changes it into vitamin D. When cats and dogs lick themselves clean, they take in vitamin D as well.

Vitamin D is rather special, because it's the only vitamin which can be made *in* the body. Just under the skin, there is a chemical which we can get from eating many different types of food. When sun shines on this chemical it instantly changes to vitamin D. Once it's formed, the vitamin D is taken away to join the body molecules and do its work.

DOG TAKING IN VITAMIN D

Vitamin D has one job in the body and it is a very important one – especially for children. It helps the body to absorb calcium. Children who don't have enough vitamin D get a disease called rickets.

Without the help of vitamin D, the body can't absorb enough calcium. This means that the bones don't grow hard and often bend slightly as they grow. A person can't die of rickets, but they have to spend the rest of their lives with arms and legs that are slightly the wrong shape. They look 'rickety'.

Countries in the northern part of the world, like Europe, Canada and the Northern United States, don't get a great deal of sunshine. Children in these countries sometimes need some extra vitamin D from their food. This can be a problem because not very many foods contain vitamin D. Eggs and milk have small amounts. Herring, kippers and fish oils (like cod liver oil) have plenty of vitamin D but fish fingers have none.

Children in northern countries are sometimes given a little cod liver oil to make sure they get enough vitamin D. Vitamin D is also added to foods. In Britain it is added to margarine and breakfast cereals. In other countries, like Canada and the United States, it is added to milk.

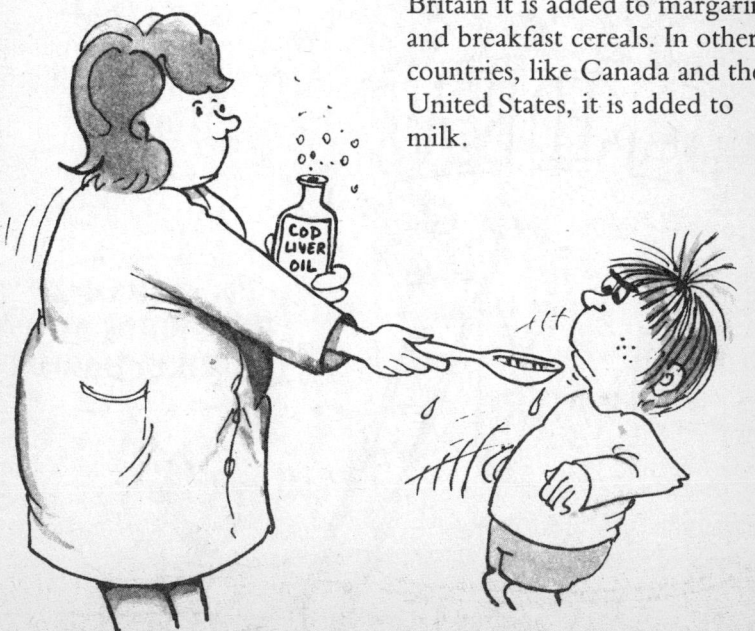

Water

There is one other ingredient in the tin of baked beans on page 9. It isn't really food, but it is very important. It is water.

Did you know that about two thirds of your body is water? You could probably survive for weeks without food, but without water you'd be dead in a few days.

It is so important to get enough water that your body has a way of telling you it needs some. You feel thirsty.

We have to keep on drinking water because we are always losing it. The most obvious loss is in the urine. Urine contains waste products from the body which are dissolved in water.

We keep cool by losing water as perspiration through tiny openings in the skin. Every time we breathe out, a tiny bit of water goes out with the air. You can see this by breathing on to a cold window or mirror.

The amount of water we lose depends on how much exercise we take and how warm and dry it is outside our bodies. It is quite easy to lose several litres of water each day.

It is very important that your body tissues contain exactly the right amount of water – but don't worry about it. Your body looks after this without you having to think about it. You just have to keep on drinking as much as you want. If you drink too much, you just lose the excess water as urine.

NEARLY ALL WATER

Most of the water you swallow is mixed with something else. Liquid food such as milk, fruit juice or soup is almost all water; so are most fruits and vegetables. Even a tin of baked beans is well over half water. Foods like roast chicken and fish fingers are over half water as well. Most people swallow several litres of water a day without even knowing it.

Why does food go bad?

There are thousands of different creatures on earth that are far too small to see except with a microscope. These 'micro-organisms', as they are called, are all around us, even in our food.

We only notice micro-organisms in food when there are millions of them. We notice if there are so many we can see them as a spot of mould on a piece of bread. Often, we can see, smell and taste the difference they've made to food – when milk goes sour, for instance. Then we say that the food has 'gone bad'.

Just as different kinds of animals eat different sorts of food, micro-organisms have some rather strange eating habits. There are micro-organisms that eat petrol, paper, and plastics. Some even eat away at the rust spots on cars. Many types of micro-organisms couldn't survive if they landed on a piece of food. But many others survive on our food very well indeed.

When one of these creatures lands on some food, it begins to absorb small food molecules. Micro-organisms don't have mouths or stomachs, but they do have digestive enzymes. Some micro-organisms release enzymes onto the food. In this way, they can digest the food outside their bodies. Then they take up the digested food through small holes in their outer skin.

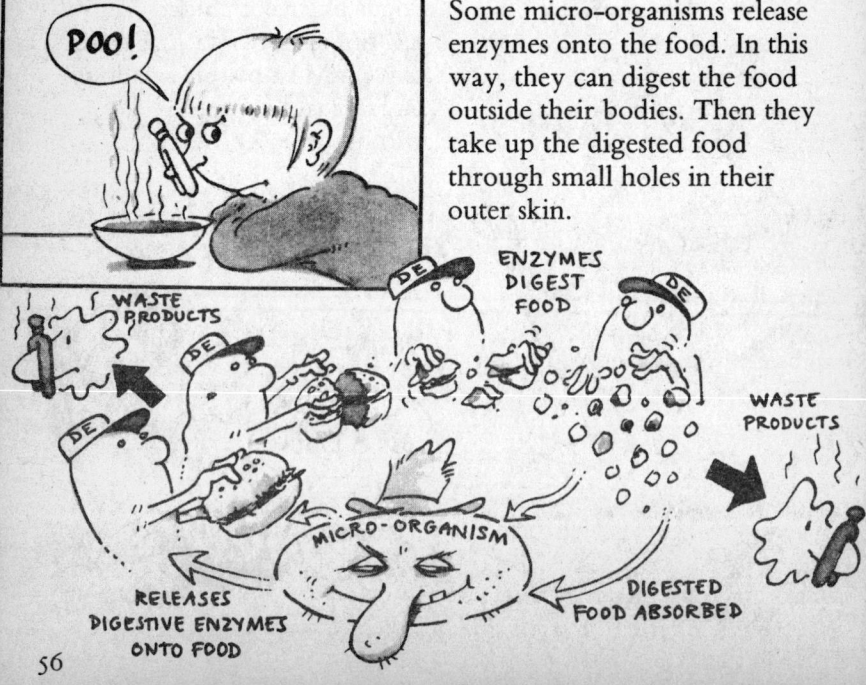

Each micro-organism grows as it absorbs the food molecules. When it reaches a certain size, it divides in two. In the right conditions, this can happen very quickly. One small creature can grow to thousands in a few hours. As they grow, the micro-organisms produce waste products. It is the build up of these waste products in the food that makes it taste and smell bad or 'off'.

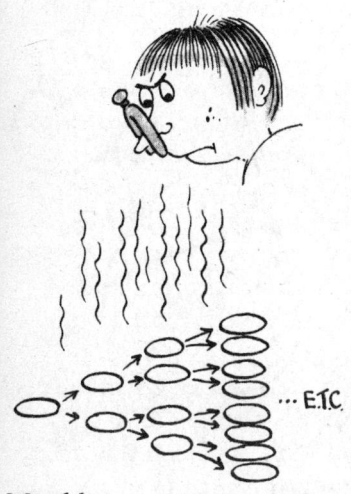

SPORES

MOULD ON A SLICE OF BREAD

TINY HAIRS

Mould seems to grow only on the top of food. But by looking at mould under the microscope, scientists have found that each patch of mould has millions of tiny hairs growing down from it. These hairs are like roots. They pick up food molecules. The bit of mould that you can see produces spores. These are released like seeds, to start the mould growing on other pieces of food.

When you find a piece of mould growing on your food do you just cut it off and eat the rest? Scientists have found that some moulds produce poisons which get into the food. So eating mouldy food can be bad for you.

Many of the micro-organisms which grow on food just make it smell and taste awful, but some produce poisons that can make us very sick. The human digestive system has two ways of stopping us from getting seriously ill from eating food which contains these poisons.

The first is simply our ability to taste and smell that the food has gone off. The second goes into operation if the first fails. The body can detect the presence of some of the most common dangerous poisons and gets rid of them as quickly as possible. This is what happens when we are sick or have diarrhoea.

How to stop food going bad

Cleaning food and keeping it clean will reduce the number of micro-organisms on it, but won't get rid of them completely. There are micro-organisms right inside many fresh foods. The air contains the spores of micro-organisms, so does the tap water you use to clean the food and there are micro-organisms on your hands.

For thousands of years, people have been looking for ways of making sure *we* get to eat our food before micro-organisms do. Many different ways have been found. They all involve either killing the micro-organisms or changing the food in some way so that they won't find it easy to eat.

Cooking food is the easiest way to kill the micro-organisms in it. Cooking won't make bad food good again, but it will kill any micro-organisms living there. None of the micro-organisms that live in food can survive high temperatures for more than a few minutes.

This is why a tin of baked beans will stay good for years. It was thoroughly cooked in the factory and then placed in a sealed tin so no new micro-organisms could get in.

All food in sealed tins or jars stays good for this reason. But it only stays good as long as the seal is unbroken. Open the tin or jar and the food will usually go bad in a few days.

There are many things that can be done to food to make it difficult or impossible for micro-organisms to digest. The best thing to do depends on the food and how long you want it to last.

Like humans, micro-organisms need water to live. If you dry food it will stay good for a very long time. Sugar, flour, rice, spaghetti, lentils, powdered milk, cereal and potato crisps all stay good as long as they are kept dry. These sorts of food are often sealed in cellophane or plastic bags to protect them from moisture and dampness.

Even reducing the amount of water in food helps it to keep longer. Grapes go bad quite quickly, but dried grapes (raisins) can last for years if they are kept in their packet. Another way of keeping fruit is to add sugar to it. Sugar makes the fruit less watery. This makes it less appetising to many micro-organisms. That's why a jar of jam can keep for months after it has been opened.

One of the best ways of keeping food good is to keep it cool. Each type of micro-organism has an ideal temperature for growing. When they get too cold, their growth slows down. The micro-organisms which live in milk grow very quickly in a warm room. They can turn milk sour in a few hours. But if you put the milk in a refrigerator, it can last for several days. Most food will stay good longer if it is kept in a refrigerator.

When food is frozen, the micro-organisms inside it stop growing completely. So freezing is an ideal way to keep food. But freezing doesn't kill the micro-organisms. As soon as the food begins to thaw out, the micro-organisms begin to start growing again. It's best to eat frozen food within a day of thawing it.

Many types of food are changed by being frozen. This isn't a problem with meat or fish, but some fruits can be damaged when they're frozen. This is why tomatoes and bananas that have been frozen are soft and squashed when they thaw out.

One of the cleverest ways of preventing micro-organisms from making food go bad was discovered many thousands of years ago. Not all microscopic creatures that grow on food make the food dangerous for us to eat. Some just change the taste of the food. They don't even make it taste bad. In some cases, if you make sure there are lots of these micro-organisms growing in the food, they will prevent the growth of more unpleasant creatures.

Do you like yoghurt? You can make it yourself from milk and a small amount of unflavoured 'live' yoghurt.

Bring the milk to the boil in a saucepan. This will kill the micro-organisms already in the milk which could make it go sour. Let the milk cool until it is warm but not hot. Then stir in a spoonful of yoghurt. Leave the mixture in a warm place, such as an airing cupboard, for five or six hours.

'Live' yoghurt is full of the micro-organisms that turn milk into yoghurt. They grow in a few hours and gradually turn the milk into yoghurt. As long as it tastes alright the yoghurt is quite safe to eat. If you like flavoured yoghurt, you can mix it with fruit.

Cheese is also made from milk with the help of micro-organisms. Before the invention of the refrigerator, the only way of keeping milk for more than a day was to turn it into yoghurt or cheese.

Today, there are many different methods of keeping food from going bad. This has made quite a difference to the sorts of food we can eat.

Peas that were picked in the spring can be eaten all year round because they were frozen as soon as they were picked. Pineapples which only grow in some parts of the world can be eaten everywhere. Once they are put into tins they will stay good – even if they have to travel half way around the world to get to your local shop.

There is one important thing to remember though! Sometimes the methods that are used against micro-organisms destroy some of the vitamins in food. Fresh oranges have lots of vitamin C, but when they are cooked to make marmalade the vitamin C completely disappears. So remember, some of the food that you eat should be fresh and preferably raw as well.

How to eat well

We are very lucky that today every food shop contains a wide choice of different foods from all over the world. Eat as many different kinds as you can. If you don't like the taste of a particular type of food or if it makes you feel sick, you should stop eating it, of course. But there's no harm in trying everything.

There is no perfect food. There is no food that will make you healthy or keep you healthy. There is no food that is bad for you unless it has been made bad by micro-organisms. (Although some people may have special health problems, so they can't eat certain types of food.) All food has some 'goodness' in it, even if it only gives us Calories of energy.

The best rule to follow if you want to eat well is don't eat too much of any one kind of food. As long as you eat many different things, you will be giving your body all the different building block molecules it needs. After that, you don't need to worry, your body knows how to do the rest.

Index

acids 29, 30
amino acids 26, 27
animals 7, 27, 31, 32, 34, 47, 51, 52, 56

bacteria 21, 27, 34, 43, 52
baked beans 8, 10, 17, 19, 24, 38, 39, 49, 51, 54, 55, 59
blood 21, 27, 49
boiling 39, 40, 52
bones 48, 53
bread 7, 25, 36, 43, 48, 49, 56
butter 42, 44

carbohydrates 31, 32, 38, 43, 46
carbohydrate molecules 31
calcium 48, 49, 53
Calories 16–19, 25, 63
carbon dioxide 15, 16, 32
cells 21, 46
cellulose 33–35, 43
cellulose molecules 43
cheese 25, 38, 48, 49, 62
chemicals 9, 10, 12, 22, 33, 36, 47, 52
chemical reactions 14–16, 21
cod liver oil 53
constipation 43
cooking 29, 30, 38, 39, 41, 42
cooking oil 44
cows 27, 33
crisps 11, 60
crystals 10, 40–42

detergent 44, 45
diarrhoea 57
diet 7, 31, 43
digestive enzymes 12, 14, 37, 56
digestive system 11, 22, 32, 34, 35, 43, 46, 49
diseases 43
dried foods 60

eggs 25, 27–29, 51, 53
energy 14, 16, 18, 19, 23–25, 32, 43, 46, 63
enzymes 12, 14, 16, 21, 37, 56

faeces 12, 34, 43, 49
fats 18, 19, 44, 46
fat molecules 44, 46
fibre (see cellulose)
fish 7, 25, 27, 29, 38, 53, 55, 61
flour 36, 38, 60
frozen foods, 4, 60, 61
fruit 4, 7, 25, 31–33, 43, 51, 55, 61

growing 12, 18, 20, 23, 48, 60, 61

health 7, 63
heart 14, 21
heat 16–18, 38
hydrophilic 44, 45
hydrophobic 44, 45

illness 6, 23
iodine 36, 37, 48
iron 49

kilocalories 17

lungs 14, 49

margarine 42, 44, 53
meat 4, 7, 25, 27, 29, 38, 44, 50, 51, 61
meringues 30
micro-organisms 27, 56, 57–63
milk 25, 27, 29, 39, 44, 48, 49, 51, 53, 55, 60–62
minerals 47–49, 51
molecules 9, 10, 12, 14–16, 18, 20–23, 25, 26, 28, 29, 31–33, 37, 40–46, 49, 51, 52, 56, 57
mould 56, 57
mouth 11, 43, 56
muscles 21, 23

nutrients 8, 22
nuts 25

oil 44, 45
oranges 49, 50, 52, 62
organs 21, 34
oxygen 16, 21, 23, 49

perspiration 54

phosphorus 48, 49
plants 7, 27, 31–33, 35, 36, 38, 44, 46, 47, 51
poisons 57
potatoes 35–37, 52
protein 23–29, 31, 32, 38, 43, 49
protein molecules 23, 26, 28, 29, 49

Riboflavin 51
rice 39, 60
roughage (see cellulose)

saliva 37
salt 8, 10, 38
scurvy 50
seeds 35, 36, 38, 44
simple sugars 32–35, 37
skin 21, 46, 52, 54, 56
spaghetti 36, 39, 60
spores 57, 58
starch 8, 35–39, 43
starch molecules 37
stomach 11, 14, 33, 56
sugar 8, 10, 20, 25, 30–33, 38, 40–43, 60
sugar molecules 10, 33, 40, 42
sweets 25, 32, 40–43

teeth 43, 48
temperature 17, 52, 59, 60
tinned foods 4, 59, 62
tissues 21, 55

urine 54, 55

vegetables 4, 7, 25, 31, 43, 51, 55
viruses 21
vitamins 50–53, 62

washing-up liquid 44, 45
waste products 21, 54, 57
water 10, 16, 28, 29, 32, 38–42, 44, 45, 47, 54, 55, 60
water molecules 10, 44

yeast 27
yoghurt 61, 62